GATE
2

Thank You!

D1466966

Happy Habits

50 science-backed rituals to adopt (or stop) to boost health and happiness

Happy Habits

Karen Salmansohn

Illustrations by Monique Aimee

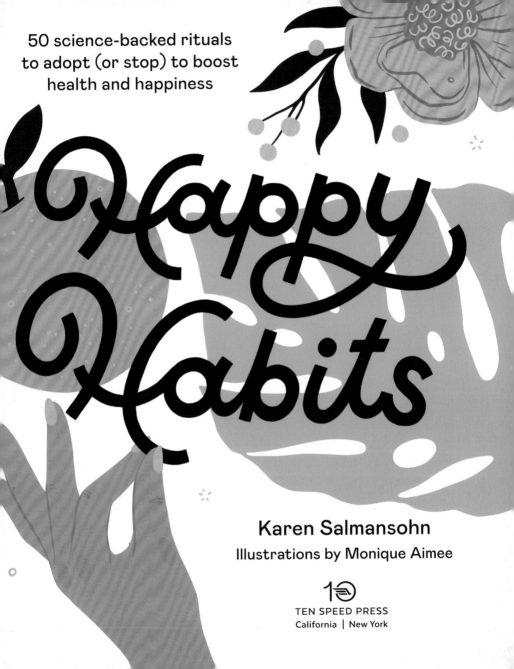

TEN SPEED PRESS
California | New York

contents

acknowledgments

I'd love to start by thanking my "Muse Team," Ari Salmansohn and Howard Schwartz, who make my heart smile every day.

Next up, I'd love to thank my brilliant editor, Shaida Boroumand, who nipped, tucked and polished everything beautifully—all while keeping my voice and message both strong and "me."

Then . . . there's my incredibly talented designer, Lisa Bieser, who is a genius at layouts, fonts, colors, style!

Plus . . . the super gifted illustrator Monique Aimee—love your gorgeous images!

And of course . . . many thanks to my awesome "agent entourage," Celeste Fine and Anna Petkovich.

Lastly, a big thank you to coffee—because without you, none of this would have been possible!

introduction:
the psychology of
habit formation

You might think you mindfully choose whatever you do on a given day—but think again.

Around 40 to 45 percent of your daily actions are actually preprogrammed habits.

So, doesn't it make sense to prep your brain with really, really good habit programming?

The better these 40 to 45 percent preprogrammed daily habits are—the better your entire life will be.

So . . .

- You need to make sure you're NOT programmed to do lots of self-sabotaging, unhealthy, unloving, negative habits.
- You need to make sure you ARE programmed to do lots of healthy, loving, successful, positive habits each day.

Because the sum of your habits has such influence on your life, in order to boost your overall happiness, you gotta tweak the habits you do most often!

No worries! I'm here to help.

The fifty habits in this book are simple, repeatable actions for you to adopt—or drop—to increase your happiness!

But first . . . I want to sneak you some helpful secrets about habit formation.

The following twelve simple tricks will make sure a Happy Habit sticks!

Yes, I rhymed that on purpose. Hey, rhyming things makes me happy—although that is not mentioned on this list!

TIP 1 **Start with Keystone Habits**

If you want to supercharge your life with positive change, it's smart to start by changing what *The Power of Habit* author Charles Duhigg calls your "Keystone Habits."

A Keystone Habit is a habit that creates such a huge change in your life that you wind up transforming your overall sense of identity. As a result, your boosted mood and self-esteem create a ripple effect into other areas of your life. Soon you'll wind up wanting to improve even more habits.

For example . . .

When people adopt habits that reduce stress, they soon find they have better focus and longer attention spans—so their work habits also improve.

When people adopt optimistic habits that improve confidence and self-esteem, they soon find they take better care of themselves overall, from making positive changes to their diets to sleeping better and having more patience.

I recommend bookending your day with Keystone Happy Habits—a stress-reducing one in the morning and an optimistic one in the evening (see "Keystone Happy Habits" on page 9).

TIP 2 **Create Positive Morning and Evening Habits**

Beginning and ending your day with a positive habit can have an awesome impact on the next twenty-four hours of your life.

For example . . .

- If you work out in the morning, researchers from Brigham Young University discovered that for the rest of the day, you'll find snacking to be less tempting, and you'll be more active in general.

- If you do a gratitude practice before bedtime, a study in the *Journal of Psychosomatic Research* found that you'll sleep better and will often wake up the next morning feeling more refreshed and in a more positive frame of mind.

TIP 3 Obviousness Is a Great Motivator

Whatever new habit you choose to embrace, be sure to make it highly specific and easily measurable.

For example . . .

Do not say: "I want to eat better."

This is basically code for: "I don't want to commit to anything in a specific way."

Say instead: "I will start eating vegetables and fruits for snacks."

Basically, when you're crystal clear about the specifics of a new habit change, you're more likely to adopt it and/or drop it!

TIP 4 Don't Wait to Be Ready

Sometimes you feel ready for change only after you start to change your behavior.

So, don't try to change your mind in order to change your behavior—change your behavior to change your mind.

There's a famous expression attributed to Martin Luther King Jr.: "You don't have to see the whole staircase to take the first step."

Just start climbing with small steps. Eventually, you will see the staircase of happy change emerge in front of you.

TIP 5 Create Habit Stacking

Habit research reports that you should "stack" a new habit you want to create alongside an already-existing habit.

For example, let's say you are a coffee drinker who wants to do morning yoga.

Before going to sleep, put your yoga clothes in the kitchen—right near your coffeepot. When you wake up and drink your coffee, you will see your yoga gear right smack in your face.

Be sure to personalize the habit you want to stack—so it's as persuasive as possible for you! Pick a habit that you already regularly do and brainstorm how to best "merge" a new habit with it.

TIP 6 Make It So Crazy Easy, You'd Be Crazy Not to Do It

If you want to lure yourself in to doing a new habit, it's sometimes best to start out with baby steps instead of setting yourself up for failure with lofty goals that require major changes.

For example . . .

Do three push-ups in the morning. *Finito.* As time passes, you can keep making small improvements. Perhaps add an extra push-up every day or so. Keep that up for a few months and you may find yourself doing one hundred push-ups every morning.

BJ Fogg, head of the Stanford Behavior Design Lab, says that if you want to create a new habit, it helps if you simplify it first. You should make the new habit ridiculously easy and quick to do. If you make the habit too difficult, you're more likely to get discouraged and stop doing it. The goal is to find a way to make the habit both appealing and conquerable, so you'll want to do it consistently.

TIP 7 Give Yourself a Zap with an App

Try setting up reminders with an app—so you lovingly nudge yourself to do your new habit.

For example . . .

- If you want to drink more water, set alarms to remind yourself to get a glass every few hours.
- If you want to walk more, keep track of how many steps you take in a day—and get competitive with yourself about improvement.

Research shows that technological nagging works!

In a study in the *Management Science* journal, a group of economists tested this with banks in Bolivia, Peru, and the

Philippines. They sent one group of bank customers a series of texts to motivate them to save more money. A second group of bank customers received no texts. Individuals who received monthly reminders saved more than individuals who did not.

TIP 8 Dosage and Frequency Matter!

More isn't always better.

You should always keep in mind the proper "dosage" and "frequency" for each new habit you take on—and do it in the right amount.

For example . . .

If your new habit is drinking water, you don't need to drink a keg every hour. One eight-ounce glass every few hours is fine.

If you assign yourself to do too much, too often, then you won't wanna do it— and then you'll feel bad for not doing it. Plus, if you overdo it, the habit can backfire and make you feel lousy. After all, you won't feel good with a keg of water sloshing around in your belly. If you want new habits to stick, getting

the dosage (the size of the change) and the frequency (how often you do it) right will keep you from getting overwhelmed.

TIP 9 Choose Habits That Match Your Personality

Researchers Layous and Lyubomirsky at the University of California, Riverside, report the importance of picking habits that connect to your particular personality and motivations.

For example . . .

- Extroverts might benefit most from rituals that involve people— but that wouldn't be as true for introverts.
- Religious people might prefer a habit with a spiritual element.

TIP 10 Swap a Vicious Cycle for a Virtuous Cycle

If you want to get rid of a bad habit that is making you unhappy, you must do a "stop and swap"—not just a stop.

You must replace the old vicious habit with a new virtuous habit.

For example . . .

When I wanted our dog, Fluffy, to stop chewing on my slippers, I gave Fluffy something "virtuous" to chew on: a yummy bone.

Likewise . . .

- If you want to stop your sugar-craving self from chewing on too many jellybeans, try swapping in a virtuous habit like knitting.
- If you want to stop your misbehaving mind from chewing on negative thoughts, try swapping in a virtuous habit like thinking of a specific positive mantra.

TIP 11 **Plan Ahead for Worst-Case Scenarios**

It's easy to come up with (b)lame excuses for not doing a new Happy Habit.

For example . . .

If it's raining, then you don't go to the gym. So, you gotta plan ahead with an if/then backup plan.

Fill in the following blanks in advance—so you're prepared for worst-case scenarios.

IF _____ happens to stop me from my new Happy Habit, **THEN** I will do _____ instead, so I can still do a form of my new Happy Habit.

For example . . .

IF it's raining out and it's harder to get to the gym—**THEN** I will work out at home to exercise videos on YouTube.

Research reports that if/then planners do far better than non-planners.

Peter Gollwitzer, an NYU psychologist, reviewed results from ninety-four studies using if/then techniques. He found significantly higher success rates for just about every goal. In one study, 91 percent of people who used an if/then plan stuck to an exercise program versus 39 percent of non-planners.

So, IF/THEN plan ahead for success!

TIP 12 Get Rid of Your Pain Softeners

If you're trying to break a bad habit, you need to become aware of the "pain softener" stories you tell yourself—and how you might be in denial.

An example from my own life: About two years after my son was born, I was still calling the extra twenty to thirty pounds on my body the pain-softener euphemism of "my pregnancy weight."

One day I got a wake-up call from my doctor. He told me my weight gain had created high cholesterol. Once I was forced to drop my pain-softener "pregnancy weight" description—I was newly motivated to drop the extra weight.

Basically, you won't have the willpower to change your naughty ways until you snap yourself out of your pain-softener denial—and face the true pain of your bad habits head-on.

BONUS TIP If you want to read all the cool articles and scientific studies behind the habits in this book, visit www.notsalmon.com/happy-habits-endnotes.

keystone happy habits

Start your mornings with meditation. Why?

Basically, a relaxed brain is a super-willpower brain.

Studies show that stress makes you more likely to do bad habits.

UCLA neuroscientist Alex Korb explains: "Stress weakens your prefrontal cortex"—which is the self-control part of your brain.

Meditation is an important Keystone Habit because it helps you reduce stress and increase your ability to choose positive habits.

Meditation gives you an impressive trifecta of benefits:

- Reduces stress
- Builds self-control
- Simply makes you feel happier

And it doesn't take long to unlock those benefits. In a study in the *Journal of Positive Psychology*, participants reported fewer negative emotions and more positive emotions after just fifteen minutes of meditation.

your essential morning meditation ritual

Make It a Habit
Start your day with (at least) fifteen minutes of meditation or mindful breathing.

Count your blessings at bedtime—instead of simply counting sheep. Why?

A study done by Dr. Nancy Digdon reported that writing in a gratitude journal for fifteen minutes before bedtime helped people to worry less and sleep longer and more restfully.

Plus, Dr. Emma Seppälä from Stanford University reported that gratitude increases optimism, altruism, social connection, and health.

Sounds good, eh? However, I've listed gratitude as a Keystone Habit not simply because it's so powerful at boosting your mood, but because it's reported to have a positive ripple effect— empowering people to do a range of Happy Habits.

your essential evening gratitude practice

Make It a Habit

End your day with gratitude. Dedicate fifteen minutes (at least) before bedtime to writing in a gratitude journal. Or silently list five things you're grateful about and think about them as you drift to sleep.

mental
happy habits

Just because a habit is good for you doesn't make it easy to do. Reframe challenging habits so they're positive, easier, and fun.

Try these four Reframing Tools!

1. **"As If" Reframe:** Get motivated to adopt a challenging habit by imagining the results "as if" you've already achieved them.

2. **Revised Time Reframe:** Convince yourself of an urgency by setting a deadline to complete a task or a short time limit to make challenges feel manageable.

3. **New Perspective Reframe:** Imagine someone awesome convincing you to do the habit. Seeing it from another perspective may help you find ways to accomplish your goals.

4. **Humor Reframe:** Give the habit a funny name! If you can smile about it, how hard can it be?

reframe the negative

Make It a Habit

Next time you catch yourself putting off a good-for-you habit that you dread, try applying some of these reframing techniques instead.

You might think it's a bit weird to talk to yourself out loud. But according to a study in the *European Journal of Social Psychology*, if you talk to yourself using the pronoun "you" instead of "I," you can help stop yourself from feeling frazzled or anxious. Plus, this second-person self-talk builds self-esteem and improves productivity.

Another study by the University of Michigan reported that people who feared giving a speech wound up calming themselves down far more—and performing much better—when they spoke to themselves using "you" rather than "I."

talk to yourself out loud

Make It a Habit

Pump up your outlook for the day by giving yourself a morning pep talk. Tell yourself: "You are a badass rock star! You can handle anything that comes your way!" Plus, prepare for that big presentation (or interview or any stressful situation) by telling yourself things like: "You'll do great!" and "You got this!"

Keep your chin up—literally.

A 2015 study in the *Journal of Behavior Therapy and Experimental Psychiatry* reported that standing up tall makes you feel a little happier and more confident. But if you slouch or hang your shoulders, you will feel more down.

In the study, folks who walked around hunched over thought more negative words—compared to those who stood up straighter.

Plus, slumping in your chair also subconsciously influences you to think more negatively—according to a 2014 study in the *Clinical Psychology and Psychotherapy* journal.

chin up, buttercup

Make It a Habit
Better posture makes you feel better. So, each time you sit down, remember to keep your body straight—not slumped. And whenever you stand up, consider this action a cue to push your shoulders back!

I often feel better after crying it out with a friend—or shedding a few tears watching a sad movie.

It seems I'm not imagining the therapeutic benefits of crying. According to a range of studies, including one done in thirty countries, crying once a week can reduce stress.

In Japan, a "group crying service" known as *rui-katsu*, or "tear-seeking," encourages people to cry as a group. One well-known workshop includes a "handsome weeping boy" to wipe away tears. This service is famous for lowering stress—and for being extremely popular.

cry it up to feel less down

Make It a Habit
Once every weekend, turn on a sad movie or crack open a tearjerker book, grab a tissue box, and enjoy a good cry.

A 2008 study published in the *Journal of Pain* found showing an emotion can make you feel that particular emotion, even if you're faking it at first.

For example . . .

- If you smile, you will feel happier.
- If you frown, you will feel sadder.

Having trouble wiping that frown off your face? A study from the University of Cardiff found that people who did Botox—and who are thereby physically unable to frown—were actually happier on average.

Want more reasons to smile? A UK study on smiling reported that one smile is the equivalent in "brain happiness stimulation" of two thousand chocolate bars.

improve your smileage

Make It a Habit
Next time you want to jump-start a happier mood . . . smile!

Video games don't just make kids happy! They make adults of all ages happy too!

Studies report that adults who play relaxing video games score higher levels of happiness, decreased levels of depression and stress, and boosted feelings of well-being.

step up your (video) game

Make It a Habit

Find a video game you love and play it whenever you need to de-stress. Make sure that it's relaxing and not too violent. If it makes you laugh, all the better. And if you can play the game with friends—and enjoy some good social interaction—you score even higher happiness points.

Warning: Play in moderation; twenty minutes of relaxing gameplay is all you need. And don't play too close to bedtime or you might have trouble falling asleep.

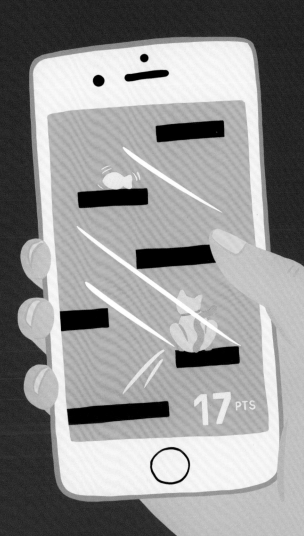

Obstacles

ARE

Temporary

When my son, Ari, was in third grade, his awesome teachers created a giant wall display honoring the word "yet"!

On this wall were a bunch of sentences, each about challenges kids might face. But instead of allowing those sentences to simmer with negativity, the teachers ended each one with a "yet."

For example . . .

- "It doesn't make sense to me . . . yet."
- "I haven't succeeded . . . yet."
- "This doesn't work . . . yet."
- "I don't get it . . . yet."

This tiny "yet" reminded kids that struggles and obstacles are temporary. With a little effort and persistence, you can push through to better results and happier times.

say the word YET

Make It a Habit
Pop a small but powerful "yet" on the end of your negative thoughts and you'll feel a lot better.

Rub, gently twist, and massage your ears all over. You'll trigger acupressure points that relieve stress and create a cascade of positive endorphins, which make you happy.

According to Eastern medicine, this practice is called ear reflexology. And it makes you feel good because it gets energy flowing all through your meridians.

According to Western medicine, this practice is called auriculotherapy. It gives you a happiness boost because your ears are packed with nerve endings—and so it stimulates your brain's reflex centers.

love up your lobes

Make It a Habit

Regularly take your thumb and pointer finger and gently rub the tops of your ears all the way down to your lobes.

relationship happy habits

Silence may be golden. But according to two research studies, chatting it up with strangers can stop you from feeling blue.

The first study, from the University of Chicago, focused on two groups of Chicago train commuters. The first group didn't interact with anyone during their commute. The second group was instructed to start a conversation with a stranger.

The group that chatted with strangers reported far happier train rides.

The second study, from the University of British Columbia, explored how customers in coffee shops felt after friendly chats with cashiers and baristas.

Customers who chatted with servers reported feeling far happier than non-chatty customers.

small talk = big benefits

Make It a Habit
Regularly start conversations with strangers—by telling them about these two studies. You'll literally feel happy you did.

Complaining—especially about pet peeves—can actually be a good thing. As long as you whine selectively—and to the right type of person—it can be a helpful key to happiness.

Says who? Robin Kowalski, a psychology professor at Clemson University, who published his study on complaining in the *Journal of Social Psychology*.

"Complaining allows us to achieve desired outcomes such as sympathy and attention," says Kowalski.

The number-one rule: You need to be a strategic complainer.

Keep in mind Kowalski's advice: "The best complainers are those who are aware of their complaining—how much, about what, and to whom. So, don't overdo it."

be a whine connoisseur

Make It a Habit

Make a list of people you consider close to you. Who in this group do you feel is 100 percent rooting for you to be happy—not competing or jealous? Who do you always feel happier after visiting—not more depressed? Schedule regular get-togethers with these people. Share some whine over a glass of wine. Don't complain for more than one glass! Be sure to ask how they're doing too—then listen!

I know, I know. You're supposed to give to others without thinking about what you get back. But Harvard University researchers report that people who charitably gave their time or money were "42 percent more likely to be happy" than those who gave nada.

Being good to others is so well known for making the giver feel good that there's even an expression for this perk: "Helper's High." The definition: When altruistic acts produce endorphins in the brain similar to a lower-level morphine high.

Why happiness happens: An Emory University study reports that helping others activates the same part of the brain as getting rewards or experiencing pleasure.

get a helper's high

Make It a Habit

Be a good human. Volunteer for a cause you care about—then show up and give back. If people you know are going through challenging times, do small acts of kindness for them— regularly. Know that when you do good, you feel good too.

Helen Fisher, PhD, a famous biological anthropologist, researches and writes a lot about why we fall in love—and stay in love.

One of her bigger beliefs about the secret to happy relationships: You must mindfully maintain a positive view of your partner, which Fisher calls "positive illusions."

Instead of spending time thinking about the worst aspects of their partner, happy couples stay focused on all the best stuff.

Basically, "love blindness" is good for the heart and happiness.

Fisher's beliefs are backed by research. In a survey of 470 studies on compatibility, psychologist Marcel Zentner, PhD, found that people in lasting relationships reveled in "positive illusions."

create positive illusions

Make It a Habit

Stop being a negative evidence collector—looking for things to complain about. Be a positive evidence collector. Whenever negative feelings about your partner start to build up, seek out things to appreciate.

You know what's sexy in a partner? Someone who answers your bids for attention. Bet you didn't see that answer coming!

Psychologists Julie and John Gottman run a relationship research center called The Love Lab. They recommend being mindfully aware of "small interactions" with your partner—also called "bids for attention" and "micro-behaviors."

For example . . .

When your partner starts a conversation—big or small—you lean in, listen, and respond with ideas, questions, empathy, interest.

One Gottman-trained psychologist reports that happy couples "lean in" 86 percent of the time. Unhappy couples do it only one-third of the time.

tune in to love

Make It a Habit
Be alert for bids for attention.
Lean in and respond lovingly.

If you can't, explain why (aka, exhaustion or busy-ness).
Apologize. Suggest another time.

Forgive them. All of your thems. The more thems you can forgive, the better you'll feel. In fact, forgiveness could be renamed "forgiftness." It's a gift of inner peace you give to yourself.

According to a new study in the *Journal of Health Psychology*, forgiveness reduces stress and increases joy.

Christopher Peterson, a psychologist at the University of Michigan, agrees. He says the ability to forgive is a quality strongly linked to positive, happy people.

let it go and happiness will come

Make It a Habit

According to researchers Julie Juola Exline and Roy Baumeister, the process of forgiveness can be experienced two ways.

1. **Privately**—with internal emotions—where you let go and release anger.
2. **Publicly**—with external behavior—where you outwardly express forgiveness.

To work on private forgiveness, whenever you feel resentment rise up within, repeat the mantra: "Resentment hurts me, not them. I choose to forgive."

To work on public forgiveness, plan a coffee meet-up with your offender, and share some comforting words with them. If you can't do it in person, write emails or letters.

Happiness is contagious—and so is unhappiness—according to fascinating research!

A 2008 study in the *British Medical Journal* reports that we can feel happier just by being around other people who are happy.

Plus, psychiatrist Robert Waldinger, director of the Harvard Study of Adult Development, agrees that people with good relationships stay happier and healthier.

His recommendation:

- Seek quality, not quantity, friendships—with happy people who make you feel happy.
- Hold out for stable, supportive, happy romantic partners—who spread their positivity to you.

spend time with happy people

Make It a Habit

Plan activities (or inactivity—aka, just hanging out) with people you feel happy being around.

Text less. Have deeper conversations more. You'll feel a heck of a lot happier—according to a study that tracked the conversations of seventy-nine people for four days.

Researchers found that "substantive conversations" with loved ones increased happiness levels. They specifically state: "The findings demonstrate that the happy life is social rather than solitary and conversationally deep rather than superficial."

So, how do you go deeper? Try "Reciprocal Self-Disclosure"— where you exchange vulnerable, personal info with someone.

Psychologists Irwin Altman and Dalmas Taylor report that when people intentionally reveal personal info (like personal desires, feelings, thoughts, private experiences), they deepen emotional connections.

stop phoning in your social life

Make It a Habit
Meet with loved ones in person more often and share more vulnerable conversations.

physical happy habits

Want to become three times more likely to feel "very happy"?

Then I recommend you stop seeing your glass of water as half full. Start seeing it as completely empty—because you've sucked that baby down!

Translation: You gotta drink a lot of water!

A study by O. Vine (done on two thousand Americans) reports that you'll snag a big happiness boost—as long as you believe you're drinking enough water.

- Eighty percent of people who reported drinking ten or more glasses of water daily were the most likely to say they were "very happy."
- Sixty-seven percent of people who reported drinking "more than enough" water (even if they drank only five glasses—which is under the recommended eight) said they're "very happy."
- Twenty-one percent of those who said they "didn't drink enough water" said they're "very happy."

enjoy h2ahhhhh

Make It a Habit

If you want to be happier, don't just focus on positive thinking. Focus on positive drinking. Drink what you believe to be enough water daily.

A study found that people who switched from few fruits and veggies to eating eight portions of fruits and veggies a day felt a heck of a lot happier. In fact, they compared their joy to an increase in life satisfaction equal to an unemployed person who found a job!

Plus, a New Zealand thirteen-day study of 405 people also discovered a link between higher levels of happiness and eating plentiful fruits and veggies. And their study participants reported:

- Higher than average levels of curiosity
- Creativity
- Positive emotions
- Feelings of engagement, meaning, and purpose

What's an especially fruitful mood booster? Clementines! A 2005 study in the journal *Chemical Senses* found that the smell of clementines made people feel "ridiculously happy."

devour good mood food

Make It a Habit
Enjoy a colorful cornucopia of fruits and veggies each day— and enjoy a brighter mood!

Being a couch potato isn't just bad for your butt (and couch), it's bad for your mood. Luckily, as soon as you boost your physical activity and heart rate—your body produces endorphins that boost your happiness.

One study reported that 78 percent of people who describe themselves as "extremely happy" said they exercise at least three times per week.

Best of all, you can exercise for as little as twenty minutes to enjoy an endorphin kick, says author Gretchen Reynolds, who has written an entire book about this, titled *The First 20 Minutes*.

get a twenty-minute endorphin kick

Make It a Habit
Find an exercise you love enough that you'll be most likely to do. If you're not sure where to start, put on some happy music and give dancing a try! A 2012 study found dancing even once a week greatly improves mood.

Sleep deprivation—according to Harvard University researchers—puts you at risk for both depression and higher levels of stress.

The solution: Take a little snooze to boost your happy mood.

The National Sleep Foundation advises that a short nap in the afternoon can revitalize you—and make you feel happier.

you snooze, you lose the bad mood

Make It a Habit

Indulge in an afternoon nap on your days off, and do your best to prioritize getting a good night's sleep each night.

Trouble sleeping? Try some holistic sleeping tools!

- **Teas:** chamomile or valerian root
- **Essential oils:** lavender or bergamot
- **Cozy stuff:** weighted blankets or soft, silky pj's

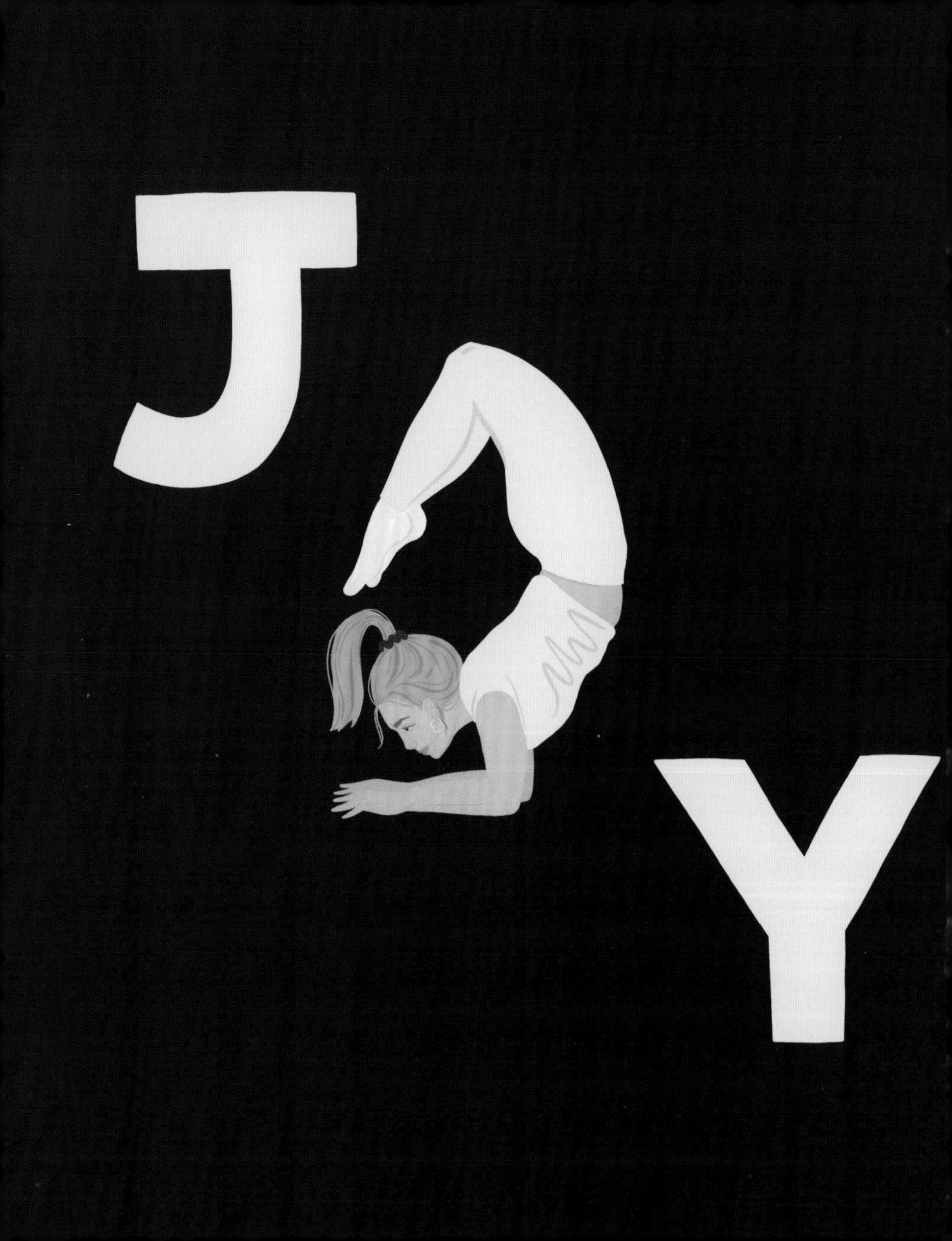
J
Y

If you're feeling down, you might want to turn yourself upside down.

In fact, studies report lots of health benefits (both emotional and physical) to doing headstands—or simply inverting your body.

- When you're standing on your head, you're sending a nice blood flow to your pituitary gland—which regulates hormones that activate happiness and relaxation.
- When you balance on your head, you breathe more deeply from your core—which is calming and good for your mood.
- When you're busy balancing yourself, you momentarily forget about those annoying stressful thoughts that were bugging you.
- When you see life from a different perspective, it's a reminder that there's more than one way to look at your problems.

headstands help you see more joy

Make It a Habit

Turn that frown upside down by turning yourself upside down. Do an inversion or headstand when you need a pick-me-up.

You might think eating something sugary will cheer you up. But it's time to think again.

"The idea that sugar can improve mood has been widely influential in popular culture, so much so that people all over the world consume sugary drinks to become more alert or combat fatigue," says psychologist Konstantinos Mantantzis from Humboldt University of Berlin.

However, in the end, researchers say eating sugary snacks will make you crash and feel worse.

According to the American Heart Association (AHA), here's the maximum amount of sugar to eat in a day:

- **Men:** 37.5 grams or 9 teaspoons
- **Women:** 25 grams or 6 teaspoons

sweeten down

Make It a Habit
Be a sweetie to yourself. Keep your daily sugar intake within the recommended limits.

A recent study reports that people who walk quickly are a lot less happy than folks who walk slooowwwwly.

But even if slow is not your style, there are a range of studies that report walking—at any speed—helps you chase away the blues.

For example, a 2014 study found that people who regularly took group walks outside were "significantly less depressed."

You don't even have to walk far to feel better. Even a short twelve-minute stroll boosted "joviality, vigor, attentiveness, and self-confidence" versus the same time spent sitting and doing nothing.

take happiness
one step at a time

Make It a Habit
Walk yourself out of a bad mood.
And know the slower you walk,
the faster you'll feel better.

In a bad mood? Get it out of your system by pounding some dough. A study, published in the *Journal of Positive Psychology*, reports that people who do creative projects—like baking bread—feel happier and more enthusiastic.

Market research by Mintel reports that 28 percent of people find joy and pleasure from baking bread from scratch.

Don't want to take time to bake? Take a whiff at your local bakery! Many studies report that basking in the aroma of bread can put you in a positive mindset.

In particular, the *Journal of Social Psychology* reported that shoppers were more likely to tell passersby that they dropped belongings if the shoppers were standing near a bakery smelling of freshly baked bread!

let bread go to your head

Make It a Habit

If you need a mood lift— knead some bread! Or visit local bakeries.

home
happy habits

Depressed? Declutter!

Studies report that people who have more clutter in their homes also have more of the stress hormone "cortisol."

Says who?

Both a 2010 study in the *Personality and Social Psychology Bulletin* and a 2011 study from Princeton University! Each reported that people who described their living spaces as "cluttered" also described themselves as depressed and fatigued.

declutter your home and your mind will follow

Make It a Habit

Don't let your stuff weigh down your mood. Find a decluttering method that works for you and start getting rid of those extra things taking up space at home. Remember: Having less stuff can bring you more joy.

Here's a bright idea for improving your mood. Open up your curtains and let the sun shine in!

If you don't get much sunshine in your home, enjoy some good sunny indoor lighting.

Certain kinds of light send signals to your body that can affect how you feel. According to Robert Cain, MD, special sun lamps for Seasonal Affective Disorder (SAD) can improve your melatonin (to help you sleep) and your serotonin (to regulate your mood).

Dr. Cain reminds us that it's important to first ask your doctor if any medication you take—or health issues you have—might make you more sensitive to light.

lighten up a dark mood with light

Make It a Habit

Sit in the sunshine or near the sun lamp in the morning while you're having breakfast. Position the lamp above you by thirty degrees. Begin with twenty- to thirty-minute sessions. If you need more, slowly increase each session until you reach sixty minutes.

If you're in a dark mood, add some color to your life!

A 2010 study in the *BMC Medical Research Methodology* journal reports a link between positive moods and saturated colors—so try adding bright colors into your surroundings to help you brighten up your perspective!

"The color yellow can lift your spirits and self-esteem," says color psychologist Angela Wright. (Hmmm . . . perhaps that's why the famous smiley face icon is yellow?)

Leatrice Eiseman, a color specialist and executive director of the Pantone Color Institute, agrees. She says, "The first words that come to mind when people see the color yellow are 'sunshine,' 'warmth,' 'cheer,' 'happiness,' and 'playfulness.'"

Color psychologists consistently suggest keeping away from grays—which are linked to anxiety and depression.

avoid fifty shades of gray in your home and wardrobe

Make It a Habit
Create a yellow (or your favorite bright, vibrant color) accent wall in your home. Or put up lots of colorful artwork. Plus, experiment with wearing more yellow clothes!

If you want to feel good, you might wanna do something that feels good. Wink, wink.

And that's a great way to start your day. "Having sex in the morning releases the feel-good chemical oxytocin," says Dr. Debby Hebernick, an American research scientist.

A University of Colorado Boulder survey reports that folks who have sex two to three times per month are 33 percent more likely to be happy than those who are abstinent.

Bonus Happiness Points: People who simply believed they had more sex than others reported higher happiness levels.

have more fun in the bedroom

Make It a Habit
Start your day with a little pleasure (by yourself or with your partner) and release some blessed dopamine and oxytocin, those famed feel-good chemicals.

The bedroom isn't the only fun room in your home. Spend time in the kitchen!

People who engage in creative activities, such as cooking and baking, when anxious wind up boosting their happiness—according to a 2016 study from the *Journal of Positive Psychology*.

Many psychologists consider cooking and baking to be therapy because they're considered "positively rewarding activities." As a result, cooking and baking up a storm helps you to deal with life's storms.

It's thereby no surprise the *Journal of Positive Psychology* study reports that subjects who were assigned creative projects (including cooking and baking) felt far happier the next day.

have more fun in the kitchen

Make It a Habit
A recipe for a better mood might be in your favorite recipe book. (Note: Just be sure not to use too much sugar as per my tip on page 62.)

If you regularly write in a journal, you'll get more deeply in touch with your you-iest you, which will then make you a happier you. It's a simple way to check in with yourself and assess how you're feeling—which might help reveal other habits you want to change too!

According to studies done in 2005 by Baikie & Wilhelm, journaling helps you:

- Process difficult events
- Create helpful narratives about challenging experiences
- Let go of negative emotions

Plus, studies show if you keep a gratitude journal (writing about what you appreciate in your day), you'll feel happier, more resilient, and enjoy better relationships.

take selfies of your soul

Make It a Habit

If maintaining a daily journal sounds overwhelming, simply commit to writing a sentence or two a day (the prompts in my *Instant Happy Journal* can help). Every once in a while, reread your journal for an extra dose of happiness.

Flying Solo

Spend some quality time with yourself watching movies, reading books, or doing absolutely nothing.

According to Matthew Bowker, a psychoanalytic theorist and solitude researcher, being alone helps people to become more resilient, self-aware, self-reliant, and self-confident—all of which creates a strongly positive attitude about life.

A study in the *British Journal of Psychology* also reports that spending time by oneself, instead of with others, can be helpful for happiness.

Bonus Happiness Points: A study at the University of Buffalo reports that time alone is terrific for boosting creativity.

solitude improves attitude

Make It a Habit
Regularly spend time flying solo so
you can soar to new, happier heights.

Fill your home with plants and flowers! Watch your happiness blossom!

A 2014 study in the *Journal of Experimental Psychology* reports that houseplants boost people's overall happiness.

And a 2005 study in *Evolutionary Psychology* reports that the happiness that flowers bring can actually last for many days after they're gone.

Bonus Happiness Points: Get yourself roses—and stop to smell them! A Rutgers University study reports those who are exposed to floral scents are three times as likely to be happy.

plants make happiness bloom

Make It a Habit
Surround yourself with greenery— place plants in spaces where you spend a lot of time. According to research, the more greenery around you, the happier you'll feel.

work
happy habits

If you want to be happier, spend your money getting experiences your soul appreciates, not things your ego revels in.

A 2009 study in the *Journal of Positive Psychology* reported that buying material objects racks up significantly fewer happiness points than taking a vacation somewhere.

Sadly, the US Travel Association reported that 52 percent of Americans are still not using all of their vacation time.

The study also found that those who planned their vacation far in advance were 10 percent more likely to take a trip.

And another study in *Applied Research in Quality of Life* reported that simply planning and looking forward to a vacation can make you happier.

take more real trips, fewer ego trips

Make It a Habit
Start planning a trip now . . . and go on that vacation knowing it's a ticket to happiness.

Although learning something new might cause stress in the moment, it also creates a boost in joy—that lingers and lasts—says a study in the *Journal of Happiness Studies*.

Bonus Happiness Points: The biggest boost in joy comes from learning a skill you pick, instead of something you think you gotta learn or something forced upon you!

On a related note: A 2003 study in the *Review of General Psychology* reported that folks who have a wide range of different experiences tend to be more positive and perky than those with a more limited life.

stretch your skill sets

Make It a Habit

Streetttttchh your way to more happiness by always learning more . . . and more. With this in mind, when you're done with this book, get another one of my books to read!

A study by Australian researchers reported that commuters who walk or ride bikes to their job—known as "active" commuting—are more productive, calm, satisfied, and joyful than people who drive or take public transportation.

The theory: Being stuck in a car, or on a bus or train, feels "stressful and boring." But when you walk or bike, you don't feel trapped. Plus, you're getting exercise, which improves mood. And how you start your day sets the tone for the rest of it.

Bonus Happiness Points: In a 2018 survey by London's *Time Out*, a shorter-than-average commute (only fifteen to thirty minutes) boosts people's happiness more than sex.

be an "active" commuter

Make It a Habit
Explore whether you can walk, bike, ride a scooter, and so on . . . even for a part of your commute to work.

If you eat lunch at your desk, you're likely to feel more miserable—and be less productive—reports a British study from the University of Sussex.

The study recommends eating lunch outside to boost your general well-being and feel better about your work.

In particular, eating sandwiches on the beach boosted moods the most. Next came lunching on a park bench in a grassy area. Both choices were even preferred to restaurants.

The researchers explained: "Eating sandwiches with the sun on your face, or feeling a light refreshing breeze, can really help refresh you and refocus your mind for the afternoon ahead."

have lunch with a side of sunshine

Make It a Habit
Stop eating lunch at your desk. Do what you can to enjoy your lunch alfresco!

Pursuing goals makes you happy, says researcher David Niven, PhD. "People who could identify a goal they were pursuing were 19 percent more likely to feel satisfied with their lives and 26 percent more likely to feel positive about themselves."

How to be an expert goalie:

- Don't spend too much time impatiently looking at where you want to be. Instead, appreciate daily progress.
- Be grateful for everything you presently have.
- Compete with yourself, not others.
- Celebrate small successes on your way to your huge success.

be an expert goalie

Make It a Habit

Make a list of the steps you need to take to reach your goal. Schedule it. Create a vision board or Pinterest page with images of what you're seeking. The more you can visualize your goal, the more likely you are to real-life your goal!

Listen to music at work to get yourself feeling happier and more motivated.

A 2013 study in the *Journal of Positive Psychology* found that people could boost their mood—in as little as twelve minutes—by listening to their favorite songs.

Researchers at Kellogg School of Management at Northwestern University specifically recommend bass-heavy or empowering music (like "We Will Rock You" by Queen) if you want to feel more confident, joyous, and enthusiastic.

Bonus Happiness Points: A 2004 study in the *Journal of Behavioral Medicine* recommends singing to boost happiness and lower stress. So, if you work at a job where nobody can hear you sing, by all means, karaoke it up!

music soothes a beastly mood

Make It a Habit
Create a playlist of your favorite songs. (Throw in some from Queen.) Grab some headphones and whistle, sing, or hum while you work!

Only 2 percent of employees in Denmark work long hours. As it turns out, Denmark is one of the happiest countries in the world (according to research from the OECD Better Life Index). Coincidence? I thinketh not!

If you want to live a happier life, try not to work excessive hours—and leave your work at work when you're done for the day.

Psychologists call this enjoying "work recovery."

I call it "watching Netflix."

Research in the *Journal of Organizational Behavior* reports that when you give yourself adequate work recovery time, you more fully release stress, fatigue, and pessimism—which creates a more positive mindset.

unplug from work after work

Make It a Habit

Work reasonable hours and try not to burn the candle at both ends. Instead, take time to light an aromatherapy candle—and breathe.

If you want to feel happier, pay other people to do the stuff you hate or suck at.

And that's not just me trying to rationalize ordering in for dinner. That's a researched fact!

According to studies in the *Proceedings of the National Academy of Sciences of the United States of America*, when you hire someone else to do stuff you don't want to do (cleaning, cooking, etc.), you enjoy greater satisfaction and overall well-being.

Plus, the research found it's worth it to spend money on time-saving services (like food delivery and housekeepers) because it "protects people from the detrimental effects of time pressure on life satisfaction."

pay for free time

Make It a Habit

Look at your budget. Explore how you can find a little spare money to fund some delegating—so you can enjoy a little more spare time.

play
happy habits

You know how being in love makes you feel happier? Well, as it turns out, being in love with your town or state, and crushing on all that your location has to offer, will also improve your mood.

A study on city happiness reported that people feel cheerier when they feel a loving connection with their city and neighborhood.

A study in Norway reported that people who did more cultural activities wound up feeling higher happiness levels and lower anxiety and depression.

Men's moods improved the most from passive experiences: visiting museums, art exhibitions, concerts, or theaters.

Women's moods improved the most from active experiences: club meetings, singing, outdoor activities, and dancing.

love your city = feel less sh*tty

Make It a Habit

Get out and about—and you'll feel better within. Take advantage of the cultural and social activities near you on a regular basis!

If you're feeling stressed or depressed, you might want to try some adorableness therapy by looking at cute videos of puppies, kittens, pandas, and so on.

A scientific study in the *Computers in Human Behavior* journal reports that virtual pet therapy can be just as much of a stress reliever as being with an actual pet.

How's that? Researchers believe people receive the same rise in happiness because the visual cues are the same—whether you experience an animal's adorableness via a video or in your home.

try adorableness therapy

Make It a Habit
If you have an allergy to kittens or don't have the time or budget to go on a safari, simply scroll the internet for the latest viral cute animal video!

Do things you love—don't just watch TV shows you love.

According to a study in the *Social Indicators Research* journal, you'll feel far happier if you spend less time watching TV and more time doing stuff you love.

In fact, the study warned: People who spent the most time watching TV were by far the unhappiest.

lose your
tv remote

Make It a Habit

Limit the amount of TV watching you do. Try to binge-watch in moderation. Or at least invite a loved one to watch with you—so the experience becomes more of a socialization thing.

If you tell someone to "Go take a hike!" or "Go jump in a lake!" you're actually wishing a lot of happiness upon them!

Yep, lots of studies report that spending time in nature is a terrific stress slayer!

In particular, a study in the *Global Environmental Change* journal suggests the very best natural mood booster from nature comes from spending time near the water when the weather is warm.

With all of this in mind, many doctors are now even prescribing time in nature as a helpful way to reduce blood pressure and boost mental health.

What's the best dosage of nature to take?

According to the *Scientific Reports* journal: 120 minutes each week.

become good natured in nature

Make It a Habit
Go for more long walks outdoors near a local park or whatever water and greenery is near you.

You know all those awe-inspiring things that make you say, "WOW!" and give you goose bumps?

Scientists have been studying this jaw-dropper of an emotion called awe. They report that awe leads to more happiness—plus better health, increased generosity, and amped-up critical thinking.

Best of all, you don't have to jet off to the Taj Mahal for the happiness kickback.

According to a few studies, you can simply watch YouTube videos of breathtaking views of the world.

Plus, another study found that folks reported a boost in life satisfaction after simply reading an awe-evoking story about being on top of the Eiffel Tower and looking out at Paris.

feel more awe = feeling awesome

Make It a Habit
You don't have to skydive or mountain climb to get the awesome benefits of awe. Simply enjoy incredible stories, music, art, or images of incredible places.

If you want to put a smile on your face, you might want to put some paint on paper.

A study (in the journal *Arts & Health*) found that people who painted creative images became far happier than people who simply tried to figure out a puzzle.

If you don't feel like you're talented at painting pictures, you can simply color in someone else's images!

Studies suggest that coloring books are an effective way to stop seeing red and feel less blue.

A study by Curry and Kasser reported that subjects who spent time coloring for twenty minutes felt a decrease in anxiety and an increase in joy.

"Coloring definitely has therapeutic potential to reduce anxiety, create focus or bring [about] more mindfulness," according to certified art therapist Marygrace Berberian.

art = cathARTic

Make It a Habit

Got the blues? Paint. Draw. Doodle. Or simply spend time coloring.

According to the *Handbook of Religion and Health*, people who are either religious or value being spiritual are linked to higher levels of happiness.

Basically, you don't need to be highly religious to enjoy the happiness benefits of honoring a higher power. You can simply believe in a universal energy or embrace any kind of faith or mantra, or meditation, that helps you through hard times.

honor a higher power

Make It a Habit

Spend time valuing your inner life—and enjoying whatever aspect of faith resonates with you. It's your pick: Say a prayer. Recite a mantra. Do a compassion meditation.

Comedian Milton Berle wisely said, "Laughter is an instant vacation."

The Mayo Clinic agrees that laughter is good holistic medicine. They report lots of research that shows laughing it up is a great pick-me-up and stress lower-downer!

Plus, a study in the *Advances in Mind-Body Medicine* journal reports that laughing at funny videos helped people to feel less stressed and happier overall.

ha-ha-ha your way happy

Make It a Habit
Go to comedy clubs. See funny movies. Hang out with your most hilarious friend. Laugh so hard that you snort— then laugh about how you snorted!

Published in the United States by Ten Speed Press, an imprint of Random House, a division of Penguin Random House LLC, New York.
www.tenspeed.com

Ten Speed Press and the Ten Speed Press colophon are registered trademarks of Penguin Random House LLC.

Library of Congress Cataloging-in-Publication Data
Names: Salmansohn, Karen, author.
Title: Happy habits: 50 science-backed rituals to adopt (or stop) to boost health and happiness / Karen Salmansohn.
Description: First edition. | California: Ten Speed Press, [2020]
Identifiers: LCCN 2020016207 (print) | LCCN 2020016208 (ebook) | ISBN 9781984858221 (hardcover) | ISBN 9781984858238 (ebook)
Subjects: LCSH: Happiness. | Habit. | Self-help techniques. | Conduct of life.
Classification: LCC BF575.H27 S34156 2020 (print) | LCC BF575.H27 (ebook) | DDC 158—dc23
LC record available at https://lccn.loc.gov/2020016207
LC ebook record available at https://lccn.loc.gov/2020016208

Hardcover ISBN: 978-1-9848-5822-1
eBook ISBN: 978-1-9848-5823-8

Printed in China

Design by Lisa Schneller Bieser

10 9 8 7 6 5 4 3 2 1

First Edition